T0368338

Poems
&
Prayers

Lloyd John Pilgrim

BALBOA.PRESS
A DIVISION OF HAY HOUSE

Balboa Press books may be ordered through booksellers or by contacting:

Balboa Press
A Division of Hay House
1663 Liberty Drive
Bloomington, IN 47403
www.balboapress.com
844-682-1282

Because of the dynamic nature of the Internet, any web addresses or
links contained in this book may have changed since publication and
may no longer be valid. The views expressed in this work are solely those
of the author and do not necessarily reflect the views of the publisher,
and the publisher hereby disclaims any responsibility for them.

The author of this book does not dispense medical advice or prescribe the use
of any technique as a form of treatment for physical, emotional, or medical
problems without the advice of a physician, either directly or indirectly. The
intent of the author is only to offer information of a general nature to help
you in your quest for emotional and spiritual well-being. In the event you use
any of the information in this book for yourself, which is your constitutional
right, the author and the publisher assume no responsibility for your actions.

Any people depicted in stock imagery provided by Getty Images are
models, and such images are being used for illustrative purposes only.
Certain stock imagery © Getty Images.

Scriptures or quotes from A.C.I.M

Print information available on the last page.

ISBN: 979-8-7652-5619-0 (sc)
ISBN: 979-8-7652-5618-3 (e)

Library of Congress Control Number: 2024920941

Balboa Press rev. date: 10/25/2024

Contents

Foreword

IIIIIIIIIIIIIIIIIIIIIIIIIIII

Hello brothers and sisters, my name is Lloyd John Pilgrim. I was born in the small fishing community of St. Anthony Bight on the great Northen Peninsula of Newfoundland. As a young child even before I could start school, I can remember wondering: Who am I, why am I here, where did I come from? When you ask the universe these kinds of questions you will get answers, but only when you are prepared mentally to receive those answers.

The answers came about fifty years later. I am tempted to say that I found a book called "A Course in Miracles" by accident, but I have since learned that there are no accidents. Those thoughts of who and what I was at such a young age, were crumbs that were left to help me find my true path. The path back to Source.

Dedication

I would like to dedicate this book to my mother and father, who are no longer with us. Father was an inshore fisherman at St. Anthony Bight and that is what he loved to do. I was lucky enough to fish by his side in my teenage years. I will always cherish those memories.

My mother it seems gave up so much to raise us six children, but I'm sure she would say if she was here that she wouldn't have it any other way. A teacher when she wed, she put her career aside to raise us. An avid reader and later in life manager of the Grenfell Handicrafts in St. Anthony. I don't think I have written a single poem without wondering if mother would have enjoyed reading it. I am sure I will recite them all to her one day:

For Ruth and Clarence Pilgrim

The title of this book is "poems and prayers" while the book will be mostly of poems I would like to start with this prayer, which is one of my favourites from "A course in miracles".

The truly helpful prayer

I am here only to be truly helpful. I am here to represent Him who sent me. I do not have to worry about what to say or what to do, because He who sent me will direct me. I am content to be wherever He wishes, knowing He goes there with me. I will be healed as I let Him teach me to heal.

(A.C.I.M T-4.XI.8:2-6)

This is my first poem "necessity is the mother of all invention" as they say, and I didn't have a birthday card for my wife who was still in bed on the Sunday morning of her birthday talking to family members on the phone back in 2018. The poem tells the story of one of our first dates. For those reading this that are not familiar with the area we are from: We are both from small towns just outside of St. Anthony about 6KM apart. The Viking was a bar about 30KM from Jackie's hometown Brehat, (we kept our wedding up there a few years after). The top of the knap, this was what was known as gravity knap. A plateau and if I got enough speed up, I could glide to the steady, which where two steep hills with a sharp turn at the bottom before the town.

For Jackie

Remember that night,
back in eighty-eight.
We went out, on
A motorcycle date.

I pulled up to the door,
beside the big tree.
Your father was shaking
his finger at me.

You said, "don't mind dad,
I'll stay out to my liking".
I said, "that's good we are
going to the Viking".

The night it flew by, and soon
it would be the end of our ride.
At the top of the knap, I shut off
the engine, to let it glide.

Down through the steady,
the moon was our light.
Picking up speed, you were
holding me tight.

The end of your drive,
I pretended to miss.
We went down on the
wharf, for a good night kiss.

It has been said that only the things that do not die are real. This does not mean that we are not real. It means that we do not know who we are. We are not our bodies.

It has also been said that while we are here in this world that we think we are in, we are actually in Heaven dreaming we are having this life.

The dream of time

While dreaming in Heaven,
this very day.
We dream of a place,
that is far away.

We dream of a world
of suffering and pain.
We chase the false gods,
where there is no gain.

Time moves so slowly,
as we all have dreams.
One sleep in Heaven,
is a lifetime, it seems.

As children of God, we
have lost our way.
Not knowing, we will
awaken one day.

As the dawn draws closer,
and death is near.
We can feel God's peace,
and we lose all fear.

The life we see, is
not as it would seem.
The life we now see,
is only a dream.

For in this instant,
the dream we can see.
Death awakens, and
again, we are free.

No fear within

Today, I will not fear,
to look within.
For there is only love,
there is no sin.

Father, I will not judge
the world today.
It would be better,
to just walk away.

Walk away from the
conflict, and all strife.
Let all the others learn,
from their own life.

We are all innocent,
in this world we have made.
It's okay to love,
do not be afraid.

The awakening

Wake up my love,
you have slept for so long.
It's been twenty years,
what can be wrong?

Wake up my love,
what can be wrong?
It's been forty years,
that have come and gone.

Wake up my love,
sixty years did they pass.
You are still sleeping,
but stirring at last.

Wake up my love,
eighty years did you sleep.
You have awakened,
from sleep so deep.

You are awake my love,
what will you do?
The time it is short,
for your brothers too.

Awaken them my love,
from dreams of fear.
Let them know of our
Fathers love, so dear.

The end of illusions

In this world, there is
a way of living.
Serene and quiet,
with eyes forgiving.

And the ones who walk
the world, as like you.
See only their own,
in all that you do.

While those who have not
yet perceived the way.
Think of you as you were,
as yesterday.

Step back from the world,
let truth lead the way.
This is the simple choice
we make today.

When all dreams are over,
time will close the door.
On all our illusions,
forevermore.

The little dream

What has happened to
the Son God made?
That He would make
idols and be afraid?

Hear then the story
of our little dream.
How we fell asleep,
and lost our esteem.

Into eternity, where
all is one.
We forgot one day,
to laugh and have fun.

A tiny mad idea
had it crept.
Instead of laughter
we had all just wept.

We were endless
no cycles of living.
We never hurt,
no need of forgiving.

Heaven is not quite
remembered yet.
The need for forgiveness,
means we forget.

We know that we must
ascend from this stage.
Forgiveness perfected,
then a new age.

The Easter poem

There was a son,
who was sent from above.
A gift from our Father,
A gift of love.

A beautiful soul, like
we all can be.
Who gave us all hope,
and set us all free.

Go forth in the darkness
bringers of light.
Holiness will guide you,
into the night.

The light has healed you
now you can heal.
You bring that deep peace,
that others can feel.

In God we all have,
A function to fill.
Go forth with forgiveness,
and do His will.

We can only learn,
as we strive to teach.
Spirit atones, as
others are reached.

What AM I

Here is the decision
we have to voice.
To end uncertainty
and end all choice.

What is choice? But
to not know who you are.
What am I? answers
seem so very far.

Surely the only thing,
that can be known,
is what I am and I
need not be shown.

For what is life,
except to be yourself.
All your doubts and
questions, are something else.

Yet if we ask, as if
we do not know, the
question means, we
do not want it so.

The final dream

Let us go daily
to that holy place.
One son to one God,
from one human race.

A hint of God's glory,
is all it takes.
We will dream the final
dream, for all our sakes.

In the very instant
we thought of war.
God made peace, it
was not thought of before.

Minds may be possessed,
by illusions.
But spirit is free,
from all intrusions.

For thousands of years,
I have lived and died.
Yet I am not in touch,
with what's inside.

And for thousands more,
I would die and live.
Just for a chance, to find
the love you give.

We seek for something,
that is deep within.
It is not of the world,
not of the skin.

For this is our will,
my holy brother.
To remember Him,
there is no other.

I am that I am

I am the one that saves you,
when you are close to dying.
I am the one that takes your life,
and leaves your family crying.

I am the one that stands by you,
and declares their love unending.
I am your mortal enemy, who's
treachery is pending.

I am the life that grew inside you,
who your love, it has no bounds.
I am the loved one that left you crying,
on the cemetery grounds.

I am everyone that ever was,
and all that will ever be.
I am the Source, that all come from,
I am the light that dwells in thee.

What the heart knows

In my heart of hearts,
I know that it's true.
That God walks with me,
and He walks with you.

In our Heavenly slumber,
while we sleep at night.
He sends dreams to guide us,
so that our path may be right.

When you look at a body,
we are not what you see.
It's just a shell that surrounds,
the real you and me.

The body is an object,
that is not here to stay.
It's the spirit that drives it,
that never passes away.

Love and forgiveness
we are here to learn.
We must practice this well,
and it's Heaven we will earn.

Endless fearless love

In the endless skies,
that are our mind.
We create our weather,
be it rain or shine.

If you choose fear,
in any of its forms.
Your sky will grow dark,
And there will be storms.

Choose love, and offer
to all your loving ways.
And there will be sunshine,
and calm peaceful days.

Whatever the weather,
our skies may brew.
I will always love you,
I will stand by you.

My grandson and I

While hunting for frogs,
my grandson and I.
On a warm rainy day,
on the first of July.

At the end of a field,
the path went through the trees.
The roses, the roses,
we fell to our knees.

Wild roses may not be the sight,
like the tame ones to behold.
But in their fragrance, they make
up for it, at least by twenty-fold.

The wafting of a hundred plants,
in that tiny droke.
We knelt there in a kind of awe,
not one of us had spoke.

From your sons, we
thank you, Father above.
For frogs and roses,
and for your love.

The Newborn

Rosie red cheeks,
and a cute little nose.
Tiny little fingers,
and tiny little toes.

There is a boost of love,
That entered your life.
In addition to the love,
of husband and wife.

By this tiny person,
who came today.
Your family has grown,
in a very big way.

When there is love in your
life, it grows and grows.
With each new child,
the river of love flows.

The prayer

*There is a well, that
runs deep down below.
From my heart and soul,
do the words they flow.*

*In quiet stillness,
kneeling at my bed.
I arrange the words,
that's in my head.*

*Now on a blank page,
my pen it does glide.
Giving form to purpose,
from deep inside.*

*The days are so long,
so dark and dreary.
My heart grows heavy,
my mind is weary.*

In peace and quiet,
I sit very still.
Patiently waiting,
for my Father's will.

Then from that well, that
runs down deep below.
From my heart and soul,
did these words they flow.

Your weary soul,
does not have to wait.
Wake up from this dream,
it's never too late.

The Kingdom of Heaven,
is all of us.
United by love,
in love, we can trust.

Treasure

*There is a place, that's
inside of your mind.
Where there is a treasure,
for you to find.*

*You will look with the
eyes of Christ one day.
See all of the treasure,
and give it away.*

*You don't have to search,
your corners of mind.
It awaits in plain sight,
for you to find.*

*Given to others, your
treasure will grow.
It's Heaven's way, not
the one that we know.*

To reach this treasure,
only close your eyes.
Think only of love,
and love will arise.

Love is a treasure,
that is waiting for you.
But it must be given,
to have it too.

Miracle principal 23

23. Miracles make time and tide wait for all men. They can heal the sick and raise the dead, because you yourself made death and taxes, and can abolish both. (note that "tax" also means "strain")

You are a miracle. God creates only "that which or one who is of surpassing excellence or merit" (a dictionary definition of miracles). You are capable of this kind of creation too, being in the image and likeness of your own creator. Anything else is only your own nightmare and does not exist. Only the creations of light are real.

You are wholly lovely, a perfect shaft of pure light. Before your loveliness the stars stand transfixed, and bow to the power of your will.

What do children know of their creation except what their creator tells them?

You were created above the angels, because your role involves creation as well as protection. You who are in the image of the Father need bow only to Him, before whom, I kneel with you.

(ACIM ch.1 p 14-15)

Grateful

I am grateful for
all these earthly days.
Grateful for you,
and your loving ways.

I am grateful, there are
warm nights again.
Grateful when you send
us, your cooling rain.

I am grateful, for the
children you sent.
We call them ours, but
they are only lent.

I am grateful, we
are a part of you.
Connected by love,
to each other too.

I am grateful for nature,
mother so great.
Grateful for change, that
is ending all hate.

I am grateful for time,
spent in this place.
Grateful for us all,
the whole human race.

Namaste

*I was reckless
in my youth.
I did not know
of any truth.*

*I did not know
what life was about.
Love and joy
I did without.*

*Then one day,
you came along.
And my life did not
seem, so very wrong.*

*For many years, we
have laughed and cried.
And though it all, you
remain at my side.*

*Namaste, means,
I bow to you.
For all you have done,
for all that you do.*

Epiphany

The epiphany of love,
what else can it be?
To have loved and lost,
and now be set free.

What is this freedom,
that I have gained?
Basking in sunshine,
now standing in rain.

Let the rain cleanse me,
wash away all pain.
Let this baptism,
bring me love again.

The love that I speak,
has come from but one.
He is my Father,
and I am His Son.

Spring

If you have lost your way,
and your soul cannot sing.
Go for a walk, with a child
in the spring.

When you look at the world,
through a child's eyes.
Everything is new,
and full of surprise.

The miracle of life,
springs all around.
The water, the trees,
and up from the ground.

Be prepared for questions,
do bugs feel pain?
And why does it all die,
and come back again?

All the wonder that's theirs,
can all be yours.
Take a child by the hand,
and go outdoors.

The wedding poem

The hush of Heaven,
holds my heart today.
We are giving our
little girl away.

May you always have
each other to keep.
May you sew loves seeds,
and its bounty reap.

May you walk with light
feet, upon the ground.
May you never let your
heart, weigh you down.

Peace to your mind, let all
your thoughts be still.
You are here to love,
and to do God's will.

Miracles

Let the miracles fall,
like drops of rain.
Grace is the gift,
that miracles contain.

The grace of God.
is an amazing thing.
When you go with grace,
it's truth that you bring.

My brothers, do not rage
against the night.
Have mercy, and God's
grace will end all fight.

Miracles show what
we have forsaken.
Time it shall end,
and love will awaken.

Love holds no grievances

To myself, if I
will even waken.
All my grievances,
must be forsaken.

We need the forgiveness,
of each other.
The ticket to Heaven,
is our brother.

To our self, we are
never to betray.
If we are to see,
that beautiful day.

Our love holds no
grievances, in the end.
Whatever our quarrel,
you are my friend.

Till we part

Death is so fleeting,
so I have been told.
No need to fear dying,
or growing old.

When our bodies are old,
and worn and lame.
We will go back to love,
from where we came.

If our last thought when
we drew our last breath.
Was only of love,
and not of our death.

Our time on this earth,
would not be a waste.
In our best laid plans,
and all of our haste.

Joy

One function shared,
by separate minds.
Unites us in purpose,
for all mankind.

For its each, that make all,
and none is best.
All are essential,
to all of the rest.

Your light increases,
every light that shines.
As your joy calls out,
to all other minds.

It's joy that heals,
all sorrow and despair.
Give joy to others,
let them know that you care.

Bring His happiness,
to all that you see.
In your smiling face,
let His, message be.

What is ego?

Belief in separation,
from all others.
No ties with God,
or any brothers.

To believe our needs,
are met though attack.
Which binds us to body,
and lashing back.

The belief is false,
our bodies are dreams.
We are one with God,
there is no other means.

A constant voice,
that will always insist.
Give it no power,
it will not exist.

Grand Design

*With our beliefs, we
keep the world in chains.
Guard your thoughts, and
only freedom remains.*

*Belief is powerful, you
have a mighty mind.
Free your future, from
what you do not want to find.*

*Here in the present,
is the world set free.
When the past is lifted,
from you and me.*

*The present now remains,
the only time.
No past or future,
just God's grand design.*

*We look at our wishes,
and think them real.
We make our own world,
and all that we feel.*

The final judgement

What I do know of this
world that I see.
Whatever I will,
will be shown to me.

IF I will to see war,
and all of the hate.
That is what I see,
there is no escape.

If I choose to see
love, and nothing else.
I will make Heaven
on earth, for myself.

It's to see a world,
that is forgiven.
The world we judge,
is the world we live in.

The path to God,
the only direction.
God's judgement is,
the gift of correction.

Fear not love, it can
wipe away all tears.
We have judged and
dreamed, for many years.

Forever His son,
limitless and pure.
We will awaken,
loved and secure.

Atonement

Bring the innocence to light, in the answer to the call of the atonement.

For what is the atonement other than the full awareness that separation from God never occurred.

*There are chains that
bind us, unto despair.
Light, is what is needed,
to see them there.*

*This light is brought
unto, all of our minds.
And this light will release,
from chains that bind.*

*And when the chains,
in the light, disappear.
There won't be anything,
to keep us here.*

This poem is a spinoff from an English nursery rhyme.

As the title suggests, the poem is a whimsical thought I had while at work. It was also written with a dear family member in mind, who has since passed.

Georgie Porgie, pudding and pie.
Kissed the girls and made them cry.
When the boys came out to play.
Georgie Porgie ran away.
Author Unknown

On a welder's whim

As I was busy
laying beads.
This whimsical
story came to me.

Georgie Porgie was
the undisputed king.
That was until Louie
the lover entered the ring.

Then all the girls
that Georgie made cry.
Suddenly they,
had a roving eye.

Georgie knew this time,
if he ran away.
The king would be Louie,
so he had to stay.

Georgie wasn't going
down without a fight.
So that's what they did
for the rest of that night.

They met the next day
all battered and bruised.
Both of them feeling like
pawns that were used.

They found common ground
and became friends that day.
They agreed not to use women,
there must be a better way.

Let us find each other,
that is meant to be.
And love,
for the rest of eternity.

Blessed are the pure of heart

A heart that was pure,
travelled the night.
To save his brothers,
to bring them the light.

Light is the knowledge,
let it fill your mind.
Extending to all,
awakens mankind.

Brothers awaken, from
the dream of night.
A new age has come,
now will there be light.

When we stand together,
led by the Son.
Power and glory, will
come to each one.

A journey inside,
to love without end.
The path back to God,
our Father, Amen.

The law of love

This is your law my
Father, not my own.
I thought to save all,
for myself alone.

I think in private,
and it comes to pass.
Our world is only,
but a looking glass.

The law of love,
is all that I will see.
Whatever I give,
will come back to me.

Therefore, seek not to
change the world you see.
Will to change your mind,
and find destiny.

The law of love,
all we need to obey.
So would I liberate
all things today.

Father, I do not seek
the things of time.
While eternity waits,
for us to find.

Only your memory,
will set me free.
And only my forgiveness,
teaches me.

The Past

This world is but a memory,
it was over long ago.
The thoughts that made it,
long forgotten foe.

Forgive the past for
it's cruel ways.
To stay in the past
is to waste your days.

Ideas about time,
are hard to change.
Uprooting the rooted,
that will feel strange.

Look at the familiar,
what do you see?
Now, without preconception,
this is key.

The past is illusion,
and nothing more.
It will take your
present, back to before.

The concept of self

The world's purpose is,
we come without self.
We bend and shape, as
we make ourselves.

Upon such a concept,
is learning built.
We come with innocence,
not knowing guilt.

This thing we have built,
it is an idol.
To take your place,
the one who is vital.

What illusion,
to walk in the shadows!
We could have peace,
instead of the gallows!

We seem to love, and we
charm and we smile.
Alas, it's only,
for a little while.

The little self,
the face of innocence.
While pretending,
that we are chivalrous.

Long suffering pity,
throughout the years.
We can't shelter love,
our face wet with tears.

The time it will come,
when images are gone.
We know not who we are,
we have been wrong.

When every concept,
has been raised to doubt.
Questions and assumptions,
filtered out.

The truth it returns,
to this open mind.
So clean and free,
no guilt of any kind.

In time we know nothing,
I Am, before.
There's no little self,
we need to explore.

Choose once again

Temptation has one
lesson to relay.
To say you're a body,
that you'll fade away.

It would set the limit
on what you do.
If you give it power,
to choose for you.

In all His glory, if
Christ would appear.
And said choose once again,
take your place here.

Would you remain in hell,
or take His hand?
Would you be bound by fear,
or make a stand?

Don't fear temptation,
see it as a chance.
Christ will prevail,
in every circumstance.

Just say: I Am,
as God created me.
I Am, His son,
for all eternity.

This is Christ's strength,
invited to prevail.
Change weakness for strength,
God will never fail.

The seed

There are no order
of difficulties.
With faith, no bigger
than a mustard seed.

When you believe,
sickness has chosen you.
This is an error,
that you must undo.

Our dilemma, is
only of the mind.
The body can only,
abide in time.

Just say: "there's no
gain in any of this.
And pain and suffering,
you will dismiss."

We are the dreamers,
of this world of dreams.
There is no other cause,
no other means.

Yield not to temptation,
love everyone.
And pain disappears,
as mist in the sun.

Real choice

The roads of the world,
do not lead within.
Pit brother with brother,
time and agin.

World roads lead to
confusion and despair.
And yet, He travels
with us, everywhere.

We are His thoughts,
that He has never left.
We are the child He loves,
held to His breast.

From Him, there is no
road, that leads away.
For how from ourselves,
could we ever stray.

For your happiness my love

Here is the answer to
your search for peace.
The key to meaning,
for dangers to cease.

The mind unforgiving
and full of fear.
Sees darkness, and finds
danger everywhere.

Seeing only sin,
and never mistakes.
Life is unhappy, for
that's what it makes.

The mind where love
is free to spread its wings.
In peace soars over,
all dangerous things.

As sin was an idea,
that was taught.
Forgiveness is learned,
and must be sought.

If I defend myself, I am attacked

We enslave the world,
with all of our fears.
Our doubts and miseries,
our pain and tears.

Our sorrows upon the
world we now press.
Attacked on all sides,
by thoughts of death.

The world in itself,
it has no meaning.
It's what we wish,
the way thoughts are leaning.

Perhaps, the world you think,
you did not make?
Another, willingly,
God's Son did take?

Yet, we found what we
looked for, when we came.
This world, and the one
we wish, are the same.

Change, but your mind,
on what you want to see.
And all the world must
change, accordingly.

We walk in armor,
doors are locked tight.
What are we defending,
with all of our might?

Without defences, we
are Heaven's light.
We are joy in the world,
our ancient plight.

Time and again, we
have come to this place.
Until we remember,
our love and grace.

Because I will to know myself: I see
you as God's son and my Brother
(ACIM)

My brother

Can what has no
beginning, really end?
When this world is seen
as your loving friend.

Before my brother's holiness,
the world is still.
Peace descends with gentleness,
that is our Father's will.

A blessing so complete,
He shines with holy light.
Takes away the darkness,
brings vision to our sight.

He heals the sense of what
you have, will turn to dust.
Our eternal light, our brother,
we can trust.

We are the infinite
thoughts, our Father made.
Before time began,
and never to fade.

The healing

Forgiveness ends the
dream of conflict here.
It is to overlook,
what is not there.

In joyous answer,
will creation rise.
If you only look,
with forgiving eyes.

Is fear a treasure,
that you must protect?
It is a mistake,
that you must correct.

God wills you learn,
what always has been true.
Cause and effect are one,
effect, is you.

A miracle calls to
your ancient name.
What is one to Him,
must all be the same.

The son of God is reborn,
with each breath.
Until he chooses,
he does not want death.

In crucifixion,
is redemption lain.
Healing is not needed,
where there is no pain.

Forgiveness is the
answer to attack.
Where attack is deprived,
of any effect.

For our ancient name,
belongs to us all.
And all are one,
who answers Gods call.

The acceptance of love

Forget not once,
this journey has begun.
The end it is certain,
for everyone.

Doubts may come and go,
and come back again.
Behind the doubts,
there is love to attain.

Do not forget that you
walk not alone.
His word on your heart,
He guides where you roam.

Illusions of despair,
may ebb and stem.
Learn how not to be
deceived by them.

We belong to Him,
we are strangers here.
Jesus will lead us,
away from despair.

Of this journey,
the end has been written.
In a great ray,
in the stars there hidden.

An ancient journey,
long ago begun.
We start again, now
knowing we are one.

For a little while,
we did lose our way.
Now a little wiser,
we will not stray.

Let's wait here in silence,
an instant more.
Kneel to Him, who
helps us, now and before.

The newborn world,
where Christ is reborn.
Always and forever,
never to mourn.

To ask the Holy spirit to decide for you is
merely to accept your true inheritance.
(Acim p. 1654 para 5)

Valentine's day

Valentine's day, long
ago in my youth.
With paper hearts and
loving words of truth.

We would brave the
cold February night.
And go to the homes
of friends in the Bight.

When we came home,
A stack would be piled.
Each card delivered, with
love from a child.

We read them all,
then read them all again.
Valentines of love,
in our hearts remain.

Days of long ago

As I write of the days
of long ago.
I feel a kind of peace,
that touches my soul.

Men had a sense
of fellowship then.
If your chore was too big,
they would all pitch in.

If there was lack in
the community of any kind.
The women would step up,
and we would have a time.

The wharf, was my favorite
place of all.
Where the old men would
gather, and tell their tales tall.

Launching a skiff,
we sang the poker song.
We will do this no more,
those days are gone.

Seismic men

Able men,
it takes two.
To make a seismic,
drilling crew.

In the late fall,
of every year.
We would say goodbye,
to all we held dear.

Pushing the powder,
and pulling the poles.
Helping was harsh,
drilling fifty-foot holes.

From daylight till dark,
we did all we could.
For when it would thaw,
we'd sink where we stood.

The bone chilling cold,
the oilfields, northwest.
Where blessed was spring,
and home for a rest.

If you find that you are not happy in life.
These are instructions from Jesus Christ on
how to bring happiness back into your life:

The decision for God

Decisions cannot be difficult. This is obvious if you realize that you must already have made a decision not to be wholly joyous if that is what you feel. Therefore, the first step in undoing is to recognize that you have actively decided wrongly, but can as actively decide otherwise. Be very firm with yourself in this, and keep yourself fully aware of the fact that the undoing process, which does not come from you, is nevertheless within you because God placed it there. Your part is merely to return your thinking to the point at which the error was made and give it over to the atonement in peace.

Say to yourself the following as sincerely as you can, remembering that the Holy Spirit will respond fully to your slightest invitation:

I must have decided wrongly because I am not at peace.

I made the decision myself, but I can also decide otherwise.

I will to decide otherwise because I want to be at peace.

I do not feel guilty, because the Holy Spirit will

undo all the consequences of my wrong decision if I will let him.

I will to let Him by allowing Him to decide for God for me.

(From Acim. P 229-230)

The power of decision

This is the only thing you need to do for vision, happiness, release from pain and the complete escape from sin all to be given you. Say only this but mean it with no reservations, for here the power of salvation lies:

> I am responsible for what I see.
> I chose the feelings I experience,
> and I decided on the goal I would achieve.
> And everything that seems to happen to me I asked for and received as I has asked.

Deceive yourself no longer that you are helpless in the face of what is done to you, acknowledge but that you have been mistaken, and all effects of your mistakes will disappear.

(Acim p 622-663)

The course's version of the Lord's prayer

Forgive us our illusions, Father, and help us to accept our true relationship with You, in which there are no illusions, and where none can ever enter. Our holiness is Yours. What can there be in us that needs forgiveness, when Yours is perfect? The sleep of forgetfulness is only the unwillingness to remember Your forgiveness and Your love. Let us not wander into temptation, for the temptation of the Son of God is not Your will. And let us receive only what You have given and accept but this into the minds which You created, and which You love. Amen.

[ACIM p 1827]

Amen and God bless.

Printed in the United States
by Baker & Taylor Publisher Services